JANE HARRISON, a Muruwari descendant, was commissioned by Ilbijerri Theatre Co-operative to write *Stolen*, about the Stolen Generations. *Stolen* premiered in 1998, followed by seven annual seasons in Melbourne, plus tours to Sydney, Adelaide, regional Victoria, Tasmania, the UK (twice), Hong Kong and Tokyo, and readings in Canada and New York. Jane was the co-winner (with Dallas Winmar for *Aliwa!*) of the Kate Challis RAKA Award for *Stolen*. *Stolen* is studied on the VCE English and NSW HSC syllabi.

On a Park Bench was workshopped at Playbox and the Banff Playrites Colony, and was a finalist in the Lake Macquarie Drama Prize. *Rainbow's End* premiered in 2005 at the Melbourne Museum and toured to Mooroopna, and then to Japan in 2007. Jane was the 2006 Theatrelab Indigenous Award Winner for her most recent play, *Blakvelvet*. She contributed one chapter to *Many Voices, Reflections on experiences of Indigenous child separation,* published by the National Library, Canberra. Her greatest creations are her two daughters.

STOLEN

JANE HARRISON

Currency Press, Sydney

CURRENCY PLAYS

First published in 1998 by
Currency Press Pty Ltd,
PO Box 2287, Strawberry Hills NSW 2012 Australia
enquiries@currency.com.au; www.currency.com.au

First edition reprinted 1999, 2000
First revised edition published 2000; reprinted 2001 (twice)
Second revised edition published 2002; reprinted 2002, 2003, 2004 (twice), 2005
This third revised edition published 2007; reprinted 2011 (twice), 2012, 2013
(twice), 2014, 2015

In accordance with the requirement of the Australian Media, Entertainment & Arts
Alliance, Currency Press has made every effort to identify, and gain permission of,
the artists who appear in the photographs which illustrate these plays.

National Library of Australia CIP data is available from the National Library of
Australia Catalogue: http://catalogue.nla.gov.au.

Set by Dean Nottle.
Cover image by Mollison Communications: www.mollison.com.
Cover designed by Kate Florance.
Printed by Tien Wah Press, Malaysia.

Contents

Making History: Directing *Stolen*

   Wesley Enoch   *vii*

Author's Note   *xiii*

STOLEN   1

Making History
Directing the first production of *Stolen*

Wesley Enoch

Jane Harrison's *Stolen* is a play that helped to change the course of history. From the first standing ovation at its Melbourne premiere in 1998 through its sold-out seasons across Australia and the world, *Stolen* found a time, place and issue perfectly in tune with the zeitgeist, and helped to galvanise support for the plight of the Stolen Generations. The play has been regularly revived in new productions, it has toured across the globe and it has been seen by almost 150,000 people. In April 2000 when then Minister for Aboriginal Affairs Senator John Herron provoked public outrage by saying that only ten per cent of Aboriginal children were ever taken from their families, the Sydney season of the show sold out within three days. The following month *Stolen* was performed during the time of the landmark walk across Sydney Harbour Bridge when more than 200,000 people turned out to show their support for Indigenous issues. It's a rare thing to be involved in a play that encapsulates a definitive moment in art and politics.

Stolen was originally commissioned by Ilbijerri Aboriginal and Torres Strait Islander Theatre Co-operative in 1992, after the success of *Up the Road* by John Harding. Kylie Belling, current Artistic Director of the company and part of the original Ilbijerri Committee, says that the aim was to create a contemporary piece of theatre that was important to the community. Ilbijerri advertised for a writer and Jane Harrison applied. Harrison and a team of researchers, most notably

Antoinette Braybrook, then began interviewing community members and devising a script. I became involved in 1993 and directed a reading of a draft then called *The Lost Children*. The title was changed when audience members argued that the children were never lost, they were stolen. This happened before the Royal Commission or any broader public knowledge of the Stolen Generations. It is hard to believe now, because it seems that we have always known it, but the general population in the mid-1990s knew nothing about Aboriginal children being taken away as part of a government policy called Assimilation. It is part of the extraordinary nature of this work and the political campaign that surrounded it that this changed.

After the initial reading, Ilbijerri spent five years trying to raise funding for a full production, and undertaking a number of redrafts and workshops in the meantime. It was not until 1997 when Aubrey Mellor, Artistic Director of Playbox, and Sue Nattrass, then Artistic Director of the Melbourne International Festival, teamed up with Ilbijerri to finance the production that it finally got off the ground.

∎

The five principal characters in *Stolen* each represent a story common among Aboriginal people:

- Anne is a pale-skinned child who is adopted and grows up not knowing she is Aboriginal. She must make a journey of discovery to reconcile her identity to her past, both black and white.
- Sandy is a young man who has been on the run from the authorities his whole life, but refuses to forget the cultural skills passed down to him from his family.
- Shirley was taken as a child and grows up to see her own children taken from her, personifying the cycle of the Stolen Generations.
- Ruby is abused and beaten as a young girl, before being trained as a domestic and eventually suffering from mental illness.
- Jimmy is a vibrant young boy who rebels against the system, is beaten and takes his own life in jail.

The journey of each character is shown by a different structure—a song, a letter, the line-up for example—which is repeated several times to show the changing circumstances and to develop individual narratives. This reflects the practice of traditional storytelling methods which have a repetitive song/dance structure. Such use of repetition not only helps in the learning of a story but it highlights the subtle changes in understanding that may occur over time. As you grow older your life experience affects how you read a story. In this sense, *Stolen* is less of a play and more of an accumulation of affecting experiences for an audience. It gives an emotional resonance to a political issue.

The brief to Jane from Ilbijerri meant that certain guiding principles were kept at the forefront, and these were passed on to the production team as we brought the show to life:

- The piece should be contemporary and unlike any other Indigenous theatre piece. We did not want it to be a naturalistic, kitchen-sink drama.
- There were to be no 'stars', it was to be a true ensemble piece.
- Traditional forms of storytelling should be our greatest influence.
- We should not shy away from the emotional power of the stories.

Developed in the script and during rehearsals were a number of symbols designed to encapsulate the experience of being taken away and the subsequent feelings of isolation this engendered:

- A filing cabinet represented the bureaucratic letters and documents that controlled and regimented the children's lives, but could not be accessed by them. Even today some people have not seen the files that controlled their childhoods.
- Beds signified the institutions where the children were kept. There was a regimented way to make them and a strict inventory of linen and bedclothes. The beds were moved about the performance space, too, to symbolise how the children were not permitted to settle or rest. Our beds should be places of security and relaxation, but in *Stolen* they were charged with uncertainty, fear and institutionalisation.
- The ringing of a bell symbolised the strict authority in the homes and missions, summoning the children to classes, meals or to line up for inspections. In the original production the bell was rung to call the children to be viewed for prospective adoption or a

weekend visit with a white family. For some children this led to abuse.

- Children's songs helped to emphasise the age of the children at the beginning of the play, and to accentuate their lost innocence and loneliness.

- Suitcases were the production's clearest symbol with each character carrying a suitcase to represent their journey and the 'baggage' of their lives, their history and their stories. At the beginning of the performance each actor entered with a suitcase. At the end, once the set had been dismantled, they exited, again carrying a suitcase to signify that their journey was not yet finished.

One of the dangers with a play like *Stolen* is that it becomes a 'stand and deliver' experience with motionless actors delivering their lines, preaching their stories. Since true drama needs action, we spent much rehearsal time searching for and developing actions and concepts that distilled the experience of being taken away. In the scene where Shirley is talking about going into the wool shop, for example, the actor held knitting needles and her long panel of knitting unravelled without her knowledge. As the audience saw her hard work falling away, they could identify the feelings of the story in the action.

Indigenous plays are a way of weaving our perspective into the public storytelling of this nation. So much of what the general public knows about Indigenous Australia comes from a white perspective, filtered through the white-owned media. Plays give us a direct way to tell our stories; to give a sense of what it's like to be Indigenous. We are not a problem to be solved, we are people with emotions and families. The universal themes of *Stolen* have been the key to its success. Audiences across the globe can identify with the need for a child to have a mother, what it means to be separated from your family, what it must feel like to be denied your culture and language. They recognise that no one should be treated as sub-human.

It is encouraging that a story so specifically Indigenous has had such a huge effect on the nation and on audiences worldwide. It shows that telling a story has the power to affect the course of history. By engaging in fiction somehow we can get closer to the facts and by telling very specific stories we tell universal ones. Maybe 'truth-telling' is the role that theatre needs to take into the future as our media become increasingly focused on entertainment and less concerned with seeking the truth; and as our politicians care more about spin than working for a community.

Theatre is a powerful medium because, at its best, drama reaches deep inside its audience and touches their souls, not necessarily to provoke change but to illuminate a side of themselves that may lie dormant. Working on *Stolen* was one of those experiences for me. Through all the turmoil and terror it has maintained my belief in humanity's generosity even in the face of extreme hardship, and my faith in the power of theatre to shift the fabric of society.

November 2006

WESLEY ENOCH is the eldest son of Doug and Lyn Enoch, from Stradbroke Island. He has been Resident Director at Sydney Theatre Company, Artistic Director of Kooemba Jdarra Indigenous Performing Arts, and Ilbijerri Aboriginal and Torres Strait Islander Theatre; Associate Artist with Queensland Theatre Company; director of the Indigenous section of the 2006 Commonwealth Games Opening Ceremony; and Associate Artistic Director for Company B.

As a writer, his work includes *The Sunshine Club*, *A Life of Grace and Piety*, *Grace*, *Cookie's Table* (Winner of the Patrick White Award 2006). Directing credits include *The Dreamers*, *Conversations with the Dead*, *Capricornia* (Company B, Belvoir St Theatre); *Stolen*, *Black Medea* (Playbox / Malthouse); *The Sunshine Club*, *The Cherry Pickers*, *Black-Ed Up*, *Black Medea*, *The 7 Stages of Grieving* (Sydney Theatre Company); *The Sapphires* (Melbourne Theatre Company); *Black-Ed Up*, *Radiance*, *The Sunshine Club*, *Fountains Beyond* (Queensland Theatre Company); *Murri Love*, *The 7 Stages of Grieving*, *The Dreamers*, *Changing Time*, *Purple Dreams*, *Bitin' Back* (Kooemba Jdarra); *Stolen*, *Shrunken Iris*, *Rainbow's End* and *Headhunter* (Ilbijerri).

From left: Stan Yarramunua, Tammy Anderson, Pauline Whyman, Kylie Belling and Tony Briggs in the Ilbijerri/Playbox production of STOLEN, 1998 (Photo: Jeff Busby)

Author's Note

Jane Harrison

Stolen had its genesis with Ilbijerri Aboriginal and Torres Strait Islander Theatre Co-operative. Ilbijerri had previously produced John Harding's *Up the Road* and was casting about for ideas for their second production. The Stolen Generations were an issue of great magnitude within the community, and that became the chosen theme. Ilbijerri placed an ad in a newspaper seeking a 'writer/researcher' and I responded. Never for a minute did I have an inkling of the impact it would have. On me. On Ilbijerri. On the eventual play's audiences.

I had no idea that the play that I would write (but not research—Antoinette Braybrook admirably fulfilled that task) would have eight years of consecutive seasons in Melbourne, would tour the major cities in South-East Australia and regional Victoria, as well as the United Kingdom (twice), Hong Kong, Japan and have readings in Canada and New York.

I had no idea that that play would have four years on the VCE English syllabus and be placed on the NSW HSC syllabus. That it would be translated into Japanese and be printed in Germany. That it would win awards. And that it would give me permission to consider myself a 'playwright'.

My desire in applying for the position was to learn how to write a play—I had a writing background but no experience in theatre. But more motivating was the desire to connect more with my own Indigenous heritage. I had grown up knowing my mother was Aboriginal, that I was, but without many of the links to extended family and community. Writing the play was a big step in my (continuing) journey home, a way of connecting with the Koori community and of further understanding my own 'longing to belong'.

Ilbijerri did not want the play to present Koori people as a homogenous people who all thought and felt the same way; they wanted it to tell many stories and not just one, and they wanted a play that wasn't a straight narrative. My ambitions for the play were to honour the experiences of those who had been stolen and for the play to resonate on an emotional level with its audience. It took six years, four workshops and many tears before *Stolen* made it to the stage. Tears—mine—because of the emotional rollercoaster the material engendered in me, tears of those who shared their stories, tears of frustration in the long road to production.

That the play made it through those six years of challenges and setbacks is a credit to Ilbijerri and its board. That the play has endured, and has had such a positive response in the years since, I credit to the powerful commitment to the play by its directors, cast and crews— the Stolen Generations have impacted their lives, in some instances directly. In each of the play's incarnations I have been awed by the actors' courage in working with material that cannot help but have a highly emotional and lingering effect on them. I must also thank the theatre companies—Ilbijerri without a doubt—and also Playbox as the original co-producers, and the venues that programmed the play.

All through the process I've been aware of the strong sense of ownership the Koori community has felt for this play—and their need for their stories to be told. I am honoured to have been part of this process.

October 2006

Acknowledgements

Stolen would not have been made possible without the generosity of spirit in those families and individuals who shared their own personal histories and gave their ideas and support. Dramatic setting by Andrea James and Jane Harrison.

Stolen was first produced by Ilbijerri Aboriginal and Torres Strait Islander Theatre Co-operative and Playbox Theatre Centre, in association with the Melbourne Festival, at The C.U.B. Malthouse, Melbourne, on 21 October 1998, with the following cast:

ANNE	Tammy Anderson
RUBY	Kylie Belling
JIMMY	Tony Briggs
SHIRLEY	Pauline Whyman
SANDY	Stan Yarramunua

Director, Wesley Enoch
Designer, Richard Roberts
Lighting Designer, Matt Scott
Composer, David Chesworth

STOLEN

From left: Pauline Whyman, Tony Briggs, Stan Yarramunua, Tammy Anderson, Kylie Belling in the Ilbijerri/Playbox production of STOLEN, 1998 (Photo: Jeff Busby)

CHARACTERS

JIMMY He's a mischievous boy. A shamed older boy. A sullen, angry adult with just one ray of hope: finding his family. Finally, a tormented man who gives up the fight.

RUBY A very young child who feels abandoned. A used and abused young woman. A crazy beyond reach.

SHIRLEY A stolen child who becomes a mother whose children are, in turn, stolen. A nurturer, the 'earth mother'. She never gives up searching for her kids, and always looks to the future.

SANDY Always on the run. Never belonging anywhere. A traveller, a thinker, a storyteller. A man in search of something who finally finds it: a sense of place.

ANNE Too young to understand why she was being taken from her family, Anne just saw that she was better off materially. As a teenager she had no desire to find out more about her real family. Later, when she did meet them, she was bewildered. Although still ambivalent about her real family, there is some attraction to 'going back', which is largely unresolved.

The play is performed by five actors who, in addition to the above roles, take on the following roles (sometimes merely as voices offstage):

Sandy's mum	Angry voice at grocery shop
Sandy's cousin	Ruby's tormentors: sleaze, lady, teenager, arsehole
Sandy's aunt	Man at bus stop
Sandy's aunty	Man at bar
Sandy's uncle	Two sisters at bar
Anne's adoptive mother	Anne's black family
Anne's adoptive father	Ruby's father, Len
Apple orchard owner	Ruby's sister
Jimmy's mother, Nancy Wajurri	Real estate agent
Dog trainer	Man insulting Jimmy
Voices of authority	Prison warden
Lady in the wool shop	

SETTING

Five old iron institutional beds alternate across the stage. The beds are the base of the five main characters, representing their homes at various stages of their lives. At times they become: a children's home; a prison cell; a mental institution; and a girl's bedroom. The covers on the beds are old, drab, chenille bedspreads, except for Anne's, which is much prettier; most of her story taking place in her white adoptive parents' home.

The only other variation in the beds is Jimmy's; his bed is turned around so the bedhead faces the audience. At times the bars on the bed remind us of the bars of a prison cell, where he spends a lot of time.

Each of the beds also has a pillow which is used as a prop in various scenes. The only other props are a drab, green, metal filing cabinet, on the far side of stage right; and Holland blinds, painted a drab green, hanging from the ceiling, which indicate the shape of the room, a triangle, with the corner being centre stage to the rear.

The main link between the five characters is that they were all 'stolen' and placed in a children's home, although not necessarily at the same time. However, in many scenes they do interact as though they were all in there together.

The 'night' scenes are in the children's home. The sounds for these scenes echo the sound of a faraway playground, children's laughing and ominous ringing sounds.

The play follows no obvious chronological order. The characters move back and forward in time, sometimes being their young child in the children's home, and other times adults. However, the play does begin with the characters as children and end with the resolution of their characters—where they are at the present moment, the end result of all that has gone before.

ARRIVING

With the house lights still up and ominous music heard, the actors walk in from the rear of the stage; each holding a suitcase, they stand diagonally across the stage. They look out into the audience, acknowledging those they recognise, their eyes searching the audience for compassion.

Then each of the actors slips into their character as a child. Their body language changes, and they speak over the top of one another and in the 'stream of consciousness' style of the very young. They talk about home, family—especially their mothers and fathers. Their voices are full of hope, but tinged with sadness. The cue to finish is:

RUBY: My mum's coming for me.

ADULT FLASHES

RUBY *rocks and sings a crazy lullaby.*

RUBY: Don't need no home of me own. Got enough to do.

    SANDY *pats the suitcase on his bed.*

SANDY: I carry my home with me.

    ANNE *straightens up the pretty bedspread on her bed.*

ANNE: My home's got lace curtains—and I've got a room of my own.

    JIMMY *gazes into the distance through the bars of his prison cell (his bed). His mood is heavy and foreboding.*

JIMMY: I'm finally gunna meet my mother.

    SHIRLEY *looks excited.*

SHIRLEY: Eh! I'm gunna be a grandmother!

It's dark and we hear sounds of a woman giving birth at SHIRLEY's *bed. Moans. Cries.*

VOICE: One more push. Big push. Keep going. You're doing great.

A baby's cry.

It's a girl!

SHIRLEY *hurries to front centre stage. She waves a little hand-knitted jumper at us. And she has a parcel. She's excited.*

SHIRLEY: I know, she'll probably get tons of baby clothes but she's gotta get something from her grandma. A new baby. I bet there's nothing like that feeling of holding your new grandchild—or any child—in your arms. The tiny little fingers. Those faces they pull...

She pulls a few baby faces. At the same time the lights rise on RUBY, *crying like a baby.* RUBY *wails, then listens to see if someone is coming to pick her up. The next time her cry is louder and more demanding. Again no one comes.*

Babies are so helpless, but it's funny, you know. You hold a new baby again—and I had two of my own—and it's you that feels vulnerable. Kate, I held you once in my arms and I didn't get to hold you for another twenty-five years.

She holds the jumper to her cheek tenderly and pauses, caught up in a distant memory.

Heavens, [*laughing with exhilaration*] why am I standing here talking?! I'm going to be a grandmother!

RUBY *meanwhile sits bolt upright and calls out.*

RUBY: I want... I want my...

SHIRLEY's *voice catches. She's thinking about the past.*

SHIRLEY: I didn't get the chance to be a mother to Kate and Lionel and now I'm going to be a grandmother!

RUBY: I want my mummy...

SHIRLEY: But this time, this time... [*She wipes away a tear.*] This time I'm going to hold my baby and never let her go.

RUBY: [*screaming out*] Where are you?

2

A bell rings. JIMMY, ANNE, RUBY *and* SHIRLEY *begin their cleaning routine.* SANDY, *with his suitcase, wanders reluctantly into the environment. He puts the suitcase under the bed. Music comes up as* SANDY *makes his bed while the others sweep and scrub the floor. The smell of Phenol wafts out to the audience. Then they stand to attention again. Another bell rings.*

HIDING SANDY

Lights up to dawn. SANDY *is sitting on his bedhead fishing.*

SANDY'S MUM: [*voice*] Sandy! Sandy. We've gotta go.
SANDY: [*reeling in a fish*] What about my fish? I've caught a beauty.
SANDY'S MUM: [*voice*] Sandy, please, be a good boy. Let's go.
SANDY: What about my stuff—you got my stuff?
SANDY'S MUM: [*voice*] There's no time, Sandy. I'll get them to send it.
SANDY: But Mum, my fish…
SANDY'S MUM: [*voice*] Sandy, run!

> SANDY *moves in a panicky fashion as if he was running away from something.*

SANDY: Always on the run.
COUSIN: When me cousin came to stay, he was crying all the time. He wanted his mum and dad. My mum tried to make him feel better. She said they'd see him soon, when it was safe—maybe six months—but he cried even more.

> SANDY *moves in a panicky fashion as if he was running away from something.*

SANDY: Always on the run.
AUNT: I tried to pass him off as one of my mob but he was too pale. One day they came snooping around—the kids were in the bath—so my little bloke, Timmy, pushed him under the bubbles 'til they'd gone. It's the only time I've ever seen a black baby go blue! I knew then that it was time for him to move on.

3

SANDY *moves in a panicky fashion as if he was running away from something.*

SANDY: Always on the run.

AUNT: Sandy stayed a while with us. The Welfare came one day and I said, 'Quick! Hide in with Jake!' So he hid in Jake's kennel. Jake was the meanest-looking dog you'd ever laid eyes on and I said to them, 'You're welcome to look around the yard for him'—but they didn't. After that I sent him to Uncle Larry's.

SANDY *moves in a panicky fashion as if he was running away from something.*

SANDY: Always on the run.

UNCLE: When I took the boy in he had nothing but the shirt on his back and a wild look in his eye. He couldn't sit still. I'd take him down to the river and slowly he'd start breathing again. We'd catch a few fish and have a yarn, and he'd even crack a smile now and then. But then someone dobbed us in, and they took him. Sad to see the boy go.

SANDY *runs around.*

SANDY: Always on the run. But I don't want to go. Can't I stay here? I haven't done nothing wrong. I wanna stay. I don't wanna go.

CHORUS: Run, Sandy!

He runs around the room as if pursued until he collapses panting on his bed.

IT RAINED THE DAY

Sounds of thunder and rain. SHIRLEY, *as a child, peeps out from under the bedspread.*

SHIRLEY: [*humming*] Rain rain go away
I'm looking out of the back of the car
The car's big and black
Mummy's face is getting smaller and smaller
She's so little I can hardly see her
She's all blurry
Raindrops, tears, raindrops, tears.

She gets under the blanket again as the thunder rumbles.

As the lights slowly come up to day, we hear a rooster crowing and we see JIMMY *crawling out from underneath a bed.*

JIMMY: Shuddup you! Bloody rooster'll get me in trouble. [*He laughs. He's crawling on his belly in a hurry to get out. He squashes an egg.*] Oh no.

> JIMMY *sneaks away from the chook yard back to his bed. A voice-over of his* MOTHER *comes from offstage.*

JIMMY'S MOTHER: [*voice*] Willy, where you bin?

JIMMY: Getting eggs for breakfast, ma. 'Cept some of them are already scrambled.

> *He laughs.*

JIMMY'S MOTHER: [*voice, sighing*] Oh Willy, Willy… Don't you get caught… The Welfare—

> JIMMY *laughs. He's invincible. He throws himself on the bed and becomes his adult, staring morosely at the ceiling while the sounds of the past echo around him. His eyes shut as the voice-over goes into an echoing sound that goes loud and soft, as though straining to be brought to consciousness from the past.*

Don't… or the Welfare… If you… the Welfare… Willy, hide! Hide! The Welfare…

> JIMMY *wakes up in a fright in the children's home as the lights come up to daylight.*

JIMMY: Willy…?

> *But it is* ANNE *who is shaking him awake.*

ANNE: Jimmy!

LINE-UP 1

A bell rings and the children line up centre-stage, front. Then they look at the person next to them and realise that they are not in the right order of lightest to darkest. They rearrange the line-up and

stand expectantly, straightening their clothes and looking eager.
SANDY *doesn't quite know what is going on.* SHIRLEY *nudges him
and explains in a whisper.*

SHIRLEY: A lady and a man are coming.
RUBY: Matron said they're gunna take one of us home.
SANDY: Back home…?
SHIRLEY: Not our homes, Sandy, *their* home.
SANDY: Oh. Do ya get to stay there forever?
ANNE: But why…?

> ANNE *is ignored as* JIMMY *answers over her to* SANDY.

JIMMY: Nah, just for the weekend.
SANDY: Oh. Do ya get more to eat than the rotten food here?
JIMMY: Christ, anything'd be better—
SANDY: Do ya have to scrub the floors…?
JIMMY: Nah!
ANNE: But why…?
RUBY: Shhhh.

> *As the golden spotlight falls on each of them in turn, they sell
> themselves in their own particular way.* SHIRLEY *straightens
> her dress.* SANDY *flattens his hair.*

JIMMY: [*stepping forward*] I make my bed real good!

> RUBY *looks shy.* ANNE *sticks her little tummy out and looks cute.
> The spotlight goes back to* RUBY. *She steps forward—she has
> been chosen. In the bright light she looks white.* JIMMY *looks
> daggers at her as they peel off towards their beds.*

[*Hopefully*] They're gunna choose me one day.

> RUBY *skips out to stage right and back in the direction of her
> bed.*

THE CHOSEN

Night lighting with only ANNE *spotlit, sitting on her bed.* ANNE's *white
parents are represented by shadows falling on to a Venetian blind or a
white sheet. Her parents and* ANNE *speak in turn but do not hear what
the other is saying.*

ANNE: They always said I was special because they chose me. That's what they always said—

FATHER: We didn't have you, Princess, we chose you. [*To* MOTHER] Do you think we made a good choice?

MOTHER: [*to* FATHER] Oh yes, she was by far the best.

ANNE: The day Mum and Dad brought me home they gave me a doll that had white hair. I'd never seen such a doll. And I got my own room.

MOTHER: There's new pyjamas on the bed. They might be a bit big— but I can buy more tomorrow. Now, Anne, just tell us if you need anything. Do you need another blanket? Did you want more to eat?

ANNE: I mustn't have been in that children's home long cos I can't remember it at all.

FATHER: It's time to go to beddy-byes now, Anne. Say your prayers.

> ANNE *starts her prayers.*

[*To* MOTHER] We'll give her the best of everything.

MOTHER: [*to* FATHER] Oh yes, a good education…

FATHER: [*to* MOTHER] My word! A sense of security…

MOTHER: [*to* FATHER] Yes! And a good upbringing…

> *They nod to each other.*

ANNE: … God bless Mum and Dad. And God bless me.

> *They all sleep.*

JIMMY BEING NAUGHTY

It's dark—sounds of crickets. JIMMY *(climbing up on the bedhead) reaches up to pinch apples from the neighbour's garden.* SANDY *sits at his feet, munching an apple. The others all eat apples as if they've never tasted one before.*

JIMMY: [*to* SANDY, *in a stage whisper*] Catch.

> *They laugh as he throws down another apple.*

SANDY: [*burping*] I can't eat any more.

JIMMY: Then take some for tomorrow. You'll be glad…
VOICE. Hey, you. Who's there?

> *The boys run away, laughing.*

> [*Yelling*] Ya bloody mongrels. I'll call the police on ya…

> SANDY *and* JIMMY *run back to bed. They all sleep.*

UNSPOKEN ABUSE 1

JIMMY *wakes up and notices* RUBY *returning.*

ANNE: Jimmy! Ruby's back!
SANDY: From her weekend visit?
JIMMY: And she's got something!

> JIMMY *watches* RUBY'*s return. The other three kids start playing the patty cake game where they slap their hands as they chant.*

CHILDREN: [*chanting*] Can you keep a secret and promise not to tell…?

> RUBY *slowly walks into the scene, dragging a doll behind her.*

[*Sing-song*] Where did you go?
RUBY: Went to the playground.
CHILDREN: She went to the playground.
What did you eat?
RUBY: Ate fish and chips.
CHILDREN: She ate fish 'n' chips.
What did he give to ya?
RUBY: Gave me a doll.
CHILDREN: He gave her a doll.
What else did ya do?

> *They stop clapping.*

RUBY: I promised not to tell.
JIMMY: Oh, Ruby!

> RUBY *walks over to her bed and sits with her doll. Lights fade to night as the children sleep.*

8

IT RAINED THE DAY

Sounds of thunderstorms and rain on a tin roof. SHIRLEY *stands on her bed and looks far into the distance. She fiddles with a tiny baby's jumper that she'd kept under her pillow.*

SHIRLEY: It rained the day they took my son. I stood there getting soaked to the skin and watched the back of that big black car and his little face, so little. It only took a few moments, they didn't say anything to me. They just came and this woman picked him up and put him in the car. Someone went and fetched my husband and he ran after the car, and he ran and yelled at them to stop—and I stood there in the rain and I couldn't talk.

> *She stands there speechless, gesturing for her husband. Her grief cannot be expressed in words. She crumples back down on the bed holding the baby's jumper. They all sleep.*

RUBY COMFORTING HER BABY

RUBY *rocks in her bed. She's humming 'Rock-a-bye Baby'. She's playing with her doll.*

RUBY: What are we going to do today, Ruby?
Let's go to the lolly shop
Ruby, you can have anything you want
Let's buy a new dress for Ruby
Oh, you look so pretty in pink
Mummy's pretty girl, Ruby
Ruby, Mummy's going to get you a big present

> *She starts to cry.*

I'm going to the shop
I'll be back
Don't cry
I'm coming back for you
Don't cry now, Ruby

Shhh
I'm coming back for you
Shhhhh
I love you, Ruby…

She rocks her doll and sobs quietly.

[*Back to herself as the child*] Where are you?

RUBY *lies down and throws the doll on the floor.*

SANDY'S STORY OF THE MUNGEE

RUBY *lies in bed whimpering. Lights fade to black.* SANDY *creeps over to her, picking up the doll on the way. He tries to give it back to her but she shakes her head.*

SANDY: Are you scared of the dark?

He asks the others. They nod.

Do you wanna hear the story of the big bad Mungee? My grandfather told me this. A long time ago there was no darkness. The yurringa [*local dialect for 'sun'*] —

SHIRLEY: But you're not allowed to say that…

SANDY: It's all right. The yurringa—that is the sun—shone all the time, day, and what we now call night. The earth was very hot and in the dry season it would make all the waterholes dry up and the animals would have to travel to the south for water. One time it was so hot that there was no water and tucker was scarce. The barra [*making a gesture to describe a kangaroo*] all bounded away and the birds flew off in such a big flock that it turned the sky permanently black. Nobody minded because it was cooler in the dark. Until the Mungee came along. The Mungee was an outcast from the mob and he was mean and he was huge. He was so huge he used to eat a whole kangaroo tail by himself—every day. He was the best hunter and could sneak up on the barra drinking at the waterhole and snap its neck with his bare hands…

All the children act out being hunters, spearing and catching animals in their bare hands.

Except when the big darkness came, there were no barra… and no fish and no goannas, cos they'd all moved on to other waterholes. The Mungee got so hungry that he came and snuck into his people's camp and stole one of the children! Then he ate him up! Munch munch munch—

The children act out eating the child.

—and he was gone! The next day he did the same. Under the cover of darkness he snuck in and stole another baby and ate him up. The mob were frightened and upset and crying. They tried hiding the children but the Mungee always found them. 'The Mungee's stealing our babies', they cried to the elders. 'What are we going to do? We can't catch him because we can't see him in the dark!' The elders thought about it and came up with a plan. They would cast a spell on him. The next day the elders waited for the Mungee, and when they sensed his presence they threw magic powdered bone all over him. It stuck in his hair and on his skin and he couldn't scrub it off. The Mungee was turned into a pale skin and that was his punishment. He would never be able to sneak into the camp to steal the children because he would be seen. And the people would know. And the people would never forget.

Meanwhile, all the other children have wandered off to their beds except RUBY. SANDY *picks up his trusty suitcase.*

[*To* RUBY, *very softly*] So, Ruby, I gotta go or the matron will skin me, but remember, it's not the dark you need to be afraid of.

She nods and goes back to her bed.

YOUR MUM'S DEAD

All the children sleep. More 'dream' images (projected slides) circle around their beds. JIMMY *whimpers in his bed.*

JIMMY: [*crying out in the dark*] I wanna go home.
MATRON: [*voice-over*]: Quiet!

11

JIMMY: When's my mum gunna come for me?

MATRON: [*voice-over*]: Your mother's not coming. She's dead.

JIMMY: [*muffled by the pillow*] She's not dead, she's not.

> JIMMY *lies forlornly on his bed. We see his* MOTHER *standing offstage, isolated, spotlit, reading a letter.*

JIMMY'S MOTHER: 22nd October, 1963. Dear Willy, they say it's for the best, but I'm missing my boy. They won't tell us where they took you, but perhaps you could write and tell us so we could come and visit you and your sister. Now try not to do nothing naughty… Love, Mum and Dad.

> *The letters are projected over his face as we hear them. Throughout we see a silent demonstration of* JIMMY *being subjected to humiliation. He's being beaten (we hear the sound of the strap being applied), he's forced to clean shoes, he's sent to his room and an old tin plate of shapeless goo, his dinner, is slid across the floor in his direction. We see the once happy boy slowly shutting down.*

2nd January, 1964. Dear Willy, Happy New Year, son. Had the family 'round for Christmas but it wasn't the same without you and your sister. I keep thinking that you would've had a nice Christmas anyway. I'm sure you're getting along just fine with that nice family they said they'd find for you. You know things are a bit tough for me and your dad, but as soon as Dad gets some work they'll let us come get you. I expect you're a big strapping boy by now. At least you're being well fed and looked after. That's the main thing. Love, Mum and Dad.

MATRON: [*voice-over*]: Just forget her.

JIMMY: [*muffled by the pillow*] She's wouldn't have left me alone, she's going to come for me, just you wait.

Nobody loves me

Everybody hates me

I think I should go and eat worms

Big ones, small ones

Fat ones, skinny ones

Worms that squiggle and squirm

Nobody wants me

Everybody hates me
I think I should go and eat worms.

As the letter is finished, the lights snap up on a filing cabinet that is violently slammed shut.

LINE-UP 2

Day lights. A single peal of the bell. The children line up a bit apprehensively, especially RUBY. *Only* JIMMY *looks expectant. As the golden spotlight falls on each of them in turn, they shrink a little.* RUBY *looks shamed.* JIMMY *steps forward again.*

JIMMY: I'm a real good boy!

The spotlight goes back to RUBY. *She steps forward reluctantly.* JIMMY *pinches* RUBY *on the arm.* RUBY *goes out to stage right back towards her bed.* SANDY *and* ANNE *go back to bed while* ANNE'*s parents walk over and sit on her bedhead.*

ANNE'S TOLD SHE'S ABORIGINAL

ANNE'*s parents are anxiously discussing something off to one side of* ANNE'*s bed while she is sitting slumped on the bed, filing her nails.*

FATHER: [*to* MOTHER] Do you think it's the right thing?
MOTHER: [*to* FATHER] I think it's for the best.

They agree, then speak to ANNE.

FATHER: Princess, we need to tell you something…
MOTHER: It's not been an easy decision for us…
FATHER: We feel we have no choice and we want you to hear it from us.
MOTHER: We don't want you to hear rumours…

ANNE: What are you talking about?

MOTHER: We want you to know we'll always stand by you.

ANNE: What are you talking about…?

FATHER: There's no easy way to tell you… You know we adopted you, Anne. We chose you at the Cranby Children's Home.

ANNE: So… I knew that…

MOTHER: Anne, there's something else… it's about your mother… she's dying and she wants to see you and… she's an *Aboriginal* lady.

ANNE: Why haven't you told me that she'… /

MOTHER: [*tentatively*] —Aboriginal?

ANNE: Alive! And that she wants to see me?

MOTHER: Oh.

> MOTHER *starts to weep.*

FATHER: We thought it was for the best. You know we love you like our own daughter.

MOTHER: We love you and want the best for you.

FATHER: Anne, there's no reason why anything should change. You only have to see her… once.

MOTHER: No one need ever know.

ANNE: *I* know. And I want to know why you didn't tell me about this before.

MOTHER: [*sobbing*] The shame…

ANNE: [*angrily*] You *should* be ashamed—

> ANNE'S FATHER *draws himself upright and puts his arm around* MOTHER.

FATHER: *We've* nothing to be ashamed of. We've always acted in your best interests! Look what you've done to your mother!

> *They walk away, talking amongst themselves. Alone,* ANNE *is so confused.*

ANNE: Mum… Dad! Mum! Dad! Why? This is a nightmare!

> *She breaks down as the lights go down.*

JIMMY *is looking out from his bed.* SANDY, ANNE *and* SHIRLEY *are sitting on their beds.* RUBY *returns, even more slowly than she had before. She is dragging a book.*

JIMMY: Ruby's back.

The kids begin their chanting and playing the patty-cake game.

CHILDREN: Can you keep a secret and promise not to tell…?
Where did you go?
RUBY: Swings and slides.
CHILDREN: Swings and slides.
What did you eat?
RUBY: Ate fish and chips.
CHILDREN: She ate fish and chips.
What did he give to ya?
RUBY: Gave me a pitcha book.
CHILDREN: He gave her a pitcha book.
What did he do to ya?

The kids stop the rhythm. RUBY *hangs her head and holds her stomach.*

RUBY: I promised not to tell.
JIMMY: Oh, Ruby!
SHIRLEY: Leave her alone.
ANNE: You're a bully, Jimmy.

RUBY *stands on her own.* JIMMY *races up and snatches the book from her. She then walks, head bowed, back to her bed and they all lie down. Lights fade to night.*

YOUR MUM'S DEAD

The children sleep. JIMMY *is whimpering in his bed.*

JIMMY: I wanna go home.
VOICE: Quiet!

15

JIMMY'S MOTHER *sits offstage, spotlit, reading a letter. She's aged—her hair is now greyish.*

JIMMY'S MOTHER: 8th August, 1966. Dear Willy—

JIMMY: When's my mum gunna come for me?

JIMMY'S MOTHER: We haven't had any replies from all our letters.

VOICE: Your mother's not coming. She's dead.

JIMMY'S MOTHER: I'm sure you're much too busy to write to your old mum with school and everything—

JIMMY: [*muffled by the pillow*] She's not dead, she's not.

JIMMY'S MOTHER: —but we would sure like to hear from you. Welfare doesn't tell us much. Your dad's crook again and we don't have two pennies to rub together, but I found some red wool to knit you a pair of warm socks.

JIMMY: She's not dead…

Each of the kids starts to cry and wail.

JIMMY'S MOTHER: Hope they fit. Love, Mum and Dad.

Again, at the conclusion of the letter, we see the filing cabinet door slammed shut. They all sleep except ANNE.

TO TAN OR NOT TO TAN

ANNE *is rubbing coconut oil slowly into her skin.*

ANNE: Life is full of tricky situations… to tan or not to tan. [*She laughs.*] Every summer I try and get a suntan. I lie out there for hours smothered in coconut oil. Coconut oil! I don't have to—I'm black! [*She laughs, pulling at her milky white skin. Then she pulls a face.*] My mother's dying and she wants to see me. My *real* mother. I just can't do it, not right now… I've got exams. I'm flat out. Maybe some other time. Maybe when I get back from my holiday to Surfers. [*She gets dreamy.*] I'm going to just lie out there on the beach and go… Oh my God!

She looks shocked like it has just hit her. She falls back on the bed.

SHIRLEY'S MEMORIES

SHIRLEY, as a child, clutches the one remaining physical link to her family—an old sepia photo album. As she traces her finger over the figures, the images are projected for all the audience to see. The chorus crowd around and try to snatch the album from her.

SHIRLEY: [*sobbing and crying out*] No! No!

LINE-UP AGE TWELVE

The kids line up in the usual way. They whisper to one another.

SHIRLEY: A lady and a man are coming.
SANDY: So what…?
SHIRLEY: This time they wanna take one of us for good.
SANDY: Like we'll be adopted?
SHIRLEY: No, silly!
ANNE: But why…?

> ANNE *is ignored as* SHIRLEY *answers over to* SANDY.

SHIRLEY: They want a maid.
SANDY: Oh. Do ya get paid?
SHIRLEY: Ya meant to…
RUBY: Shhh.

> RUBY *is picked and she steps forward, only to get a mop and bucket crashing into her arms from above.*

CLEANING ROUTINE 2

They all start their cleaning routine.

RUBY: [*sarcastically*] And what are you going to be when you grow up?

> *The children call out together and mime the actions to go with the profession.*

CHILD: A nurse!
AUTHORITY FIGURE: No.
CHILD: A fireman!
AUTHORITY FIGURE: No.
CHILD: A circus performer!
AUTHORITY FIGURE: No.
CHILD: A doctor!
AUTHORITY FIGURE: No.
CHILD: A builder!
AUTHORITY FIGURE: No.
CHILD: A movie star!
AUTHORITY FIGURE: No.
CHILD: A bus driver!
AUTHORITY FIGURE: No.
CHILD: A farmer!
AUTHORITY FIGURE: No.
CHILD: A teacher.
AUTHORITY FIGURE: No.
CHILD: A domestic?
AUTHORITY FIGURE: Yes!

> *The children—except for* RUBY—*start to dance around singing
> to the tune of 'We're happy little Vegemites'.*

CHILDREN: We're training to be doctors—no
> We're training to be cooks—yes, yes
> We're training to be engineers—no
> Reading all our books—no, no, no
> We're training to be cleaners—yes
> And we'll earn much less
> Because we love to work like slaves, we all adore to work like
> slaves. It puts a rose in every cheek.

> *The children slap each other's faces.*

> We're training to be stockman—yes
> We're training to fly planes—no, no, no
> Training to be cleaners—yes
> And we'll dig the drains—yes, yes, yes
> Training to take washing in—yes
> And we'll earn much less

Because we love to work like slaves, we all adore to work like slaves. It puts a rose in every cheek. It puts a rose in every cheek!

RUBY *continues to mop.*

RUBY: Sorry, ma'am.

SHIRLEY KNITS FOR HER FAMILY

SHIRLEY *has a big bag of knitting that she lays out—from small garments to large, representing the years that she has knitted for her family without ever getting the chance to give them her symbols of love.* SHIRLEY *addresses the audience.*

SHIRLEY: I was in at the wool shop the other day and the lady says…
VOICE: [*off*] Shirley, you're always knitting.
SHIRLEY: And I said, well I've got two kids and who knows how many grandchildren. And she said…
VOICE: [*off*] Truly, how many grandchildren have you got?
SHIRLEY: I don't know… I don't know… [*She addresses the audience.*] I had to leave the shop. After all these years to get used to it, it still hurts.

In the fading light all you can hear is the clicking of her needles.

A CAN OF PEAS

The sound turns into the sound of a can being rolled backwards and forwards across the floor. The spotlight goes up on SANDY, *holding a can of peas. Throughout he builds a pyramid of the cans.*

SANDY: Can of peas. I hate peas. Some people hate bloody spinach or pumpkin, but I hate peas. Always have. You want me to tell you why? When Mum was real desperate she'd scrounge shit like this from the Welfare. White flour, white sugar, white bread. No good. Instant mash potato. Stuck to ya mouth like glue. Tinned camp pie. The stink! Like bloody dog meat. But the cans of peas I hated most. Just looking at the bloody can, I can taste them. Slimy. Soggy. Yuk. A can of peas. A can like this one ruined my family. True, a can of peas. Destroyed my mother and us kids. Mum didn't steal it or nothin' like that—she wasn't shoved in jail or anything. And it's not what you're thinking, she didn't chuck it at someone and kill 'em—though she must have wanted to. It was just when *they* finally caught up with us, a can just like this little old one was sitting way at the back of the cupboard—past its use-by date—so they said she was an unfit mother and they took us kids away. All because of a use-by date. The bloody Welfare, who gave us the rotten can in the first place. A can of peas.

He throws it up in the air and makes no attempt to catch it. It crashes noisily to the stage. He kicks the rest of the cans over.

JIMMY'S BEING NAUGHTY AGAIN

A crash of cans. JIMMY *sneaks in, grabs the cans and loads them into the box, looking guiltily around all the time.*

VOICE: [*angrily*] Who's back there?

> *The spotlight catches* JIMMY *in the process of running off with the box.*

You black bastards! I'll call the cops…

> JIMMY *laughs, but it's more an angry laugh. He races back to his bed.*

LINE-UP 3

The bell rings and the children line up sorrowfully, except for JIMMY *who's in the dark about what happens when the white family take home a child for the weekend.* RUBY *is wooden and stiff.* SHIRLEY *sneers.* SANDY *looks terrified.* ANNE *picks her nose and dirties her face.*

20

JIMMY: I do what I'm told!

> SHIRLEY *tries quietly and urgently to dissuade* JIMMY.

SHIRLEY: Jimmy, you don't want to go to *their* home—

JIMMY: Shut up! Ruby gets treats, don't she? Ruby gets good food to eat—

SHIRLEY: But—

> *This time the spotlight goes back to* JIMMY *and he steps forward happily.*

JIMMY: [*happy*] I knew it!!

> *He travels the path that* RUBY *does, but when the lights fade he goes back to his bed.*

SHIRLEY NEVER GIVES UP SEARCHING

SHIRLEY *gets on the phone and speaks.*

SHIRLEY: Yes, I'm ringing about one of my children, Lionel, who was taken from me in 1966 when he was just two years old. Why was he taken? Well, you tell me…

> *One by one all the others join her on the bed and they all make calls—to the authorities, social services, anyone who might know anything regarding the whereabouts of her children. The voices crowd over one another so it becomes a wall of sound.*

VOICE: Yes, I hope you can help me. My name is Shirley Thomas and I'm searching for my son Lionel…

VOICE: Hello, I spoke to you some time back about my son Lionel… I know you don't hold records from back then but…

VOICE: I'm just following up in the hope that you might know of an Aboriginal boy who was adopted or fostered in 1966 by a white family in your area. His name was Lionel…

VOICE: Look, I've been trying to find out about my son Lionel… He was taken with his sister…

> *After a minute of talking over one another they end their calls.* SHIRLEY *stands isolated, spotlit.*

SHIRLEY: Put me on hold…? [*She laughs bitterly.*] You people have been putting me on hold for twenty-seven years…

The others go back to their beds and sleep.

DESERT SANDS

RUBY *is whimpering in bed. The sound wakes up* SANDY *and he climbs up on his bedhead and calls for the other kids in the home to come closer. He's telling them a story.*

SANDY: My people are from the desert. Home of the red sands. When I was a little boy, my mother would tell me the story of how the desert sands were created, a long time ago. Our people were very vain. Neighbouring mob were coming over for a visit and my ancestors wanted our land to look better than anyone else's. The boss man said, 'We will build a special meeting place circled by big red rocks, the biggest rocks we can find.'

The chorus become the big red rocks.

So the men searched and found these big red rocks and they rolled them into a big circle. When the neighbouring nation came over they said, 'Very magic spot.' But then banga—the Old Wind— [*Aside to* JIMMY] Jimmy, you be banga—The Old Wind high up in the sky was blowing by and he saw what my people had done to fool their neighbours and he laughed and laughed at them. He laughed and he roared around the rocks and they all crumbled into sand and blew all over, until the land, he was covered in red sand.

The others act out being the whirling, swirling sand, until they spin slowly back in the direction of their beds.

That's how the desert sands were created. My mum used to laugh 'n laugh at that story. She was always laughing, my old mum. Had a sense of humour.

The kids creep back into their beds and SANDY *is left to finish his story alone.*

She used to say that when you walk on the sand, the wind can blow away your footsteps, like you had never made them, and the earth would become pure again. The sand could heal itself. The land where my people come from is covered in red sand and in the old days, the women, to try and stop the white men from raping them, would shove sand inside themselves. Anything to stop the men from raping them, anything. [*He becomes quieter.*] And that's what my mother did, but it didn't stop them and so I came along. My mother, she loved me, but she called me Sandy anyway. She sure had a sense of humour, that one.

Lights fade to black.

UNSPOKEN ABUSE 3

RUBY *sits and observes* JIMMY *returning. She makes a gesture so the others can see him. The other three begin the patty-cake game.*

CHILDREN: [*chanting together*] Can you keep a secret and promise not to tell?

JIMMY *slowly walks around to centre stage, holding a ball stiffly.*

[*Sing-song*] Where did you go?

JIMMY *says nothing.*

He went to the circus.
What did you eat?

JIMMY *says nothing.*

He ate pie and chips.
What did he give to ya?

JIMMY *says nothing.*

He gave him a ball.
What did he do to ya?

JIMMY *can't answer for shame.*

He promised not to tell.

He just hangs his head and goes slowly over to his bed and lies face down. SHIRLEY *tentatively goes up to the bed and goes as if to put her arm around him but just stops short. The lights fade as they sleep.*

RUBY *stands there, copping abuse. She gets a black eye smeared onto her (by the actor playing* ANNE*), her dressed ripped (by the actor playing* SHIRLEY*) and kneed in the stomach (by the actor playing* JIMMY*). Blood appears on her dress.*

AUTHORITY FIGURE: Clean for me, Ruby.
AUTHORITY FIGURE: Wash for me, Ruby.
AUTHORITY FIGURE: Cook for me, Ruby.
RUBY: Don't need no family of me own.
AUTHORITY FIGURE: Scrub for me, Ruby.
AUTHORITY FIGURE: Nurse for me, Ruby.
AUTHORITY FIGURE: Mop for me, Ruby.
RUBY: Got enough to do.
AUTHORITY FIGURE: Shop for me, Ruby.
RUBY: Don't come crying to me with ya troubles.
AUTHORITY FIGURE: Iron for me, Ruby.
RUBY: I've got enough to do.
AUTHORITY FIGURE: Do it for me, Ruby.
RUBY: Don't want no trouble.

> *All the voices crowd in on her. They get more nasty in their tone.*

SLEAZE: Wash my boots for me, Ruby.
LADY: Ruby, dear, next time can you do it the way I asked?
TEENAGER: Ruby, where's my dress?
ARSEHOLE: You're hopeless, you are.
LADY: You do try *so* hard.
ARSEHOLE: Lie down on the bloody bed.
SLEAZE: And the other boot. Scrub them, bitch.

> *He grabs the back of her head when she scrubs beneath him. The gesture is sexual.*

TEENAGER: Where's my dress? Ruby!
ARSEHOLE: You're bloody lucky that I even bother with you.
LADY: Oh Ruby, Ruby, how many times have I told you?
SLEAZE: And the back of my boots.

LADY: You've *almost* got it, Ruby.

ARSEHOLE: You dirty Abo…

SLEAZE: You missed a spot.

> RUBY *stands front centre stage and wipes at her body obsessively.*

RUBY: [*screaming*] Where are you?

> *She falls to the floor, where she huddles, rocking. We hear the sound of an ambulance siren as a red flashing light flickers around the stage, picking up her grimacing face in its beam. The lights go down. All is silent.*

SANDY'S LIFE ON THE ROAD

SANDY *is at the bus stop with his trusty suitcase. A* WOMAN *is also waiting with her shopping bag full of presents and, as they are the only people waiting, he instigates a conversation.*

SANDY: G'day, how are you?

WOMAN: Good thanks. On your way home for Christmas?

SANDY: Not likely. Never spent Christmas in the same town twice. [*He sits on his case as he settles in to tell his life story.*] Spent '58 in Swan Hill. That was a hot one. Picking grapes. That was my first year out.

> *He sees the look of fear on the* WOMAN*'s face.*

No, not out of the slammer. Though it was kind of—the children's home. I was seventeen. '59 found me west of Dubbo. Droving cattle. Didn't see another bloke for weeks. Christmas dinner was a couple of spuds on the fire and a fresh rabbit that year. Where was I in '60? That's right, on the coast. Thought I'd try my hand on a trawler, headed for up north. '61 was a good year—a bucket of prawns, fresh as could be! Long way from home but—I was way out at sea. On the boat for the next eight years, till I finally got jack of the boss. Not paying me as much as the next man, though I worked twice as hard. Next couple of years I tried my hand at a timber mill, up in the hinterland. Built a humpy on the

25

outskirts of town, thought I'd settle down. Maybe get myself a family… But the coppers moved me on, moved me on—

WOMAN: I'm sorry.

She rushes up and gives him a twenty-dollar note. He looks at it amused.

JIMMY'S STORY

JIMMY reaches under his bed to bring out a duffle bag. While JIMMY is packing it (his pillow) we hear his MOTHER reading another letter.

JIMMY'S MOTHER [*voice-over*]: Third of June, 1968. I am writing again to let you know that we would like our son Willy to come back home now. My husband has a job that's steady on a big property owned by Mr Jacobs and I'm taking in washing. I have written to the lady that took Willy, her name was Mrs Mead, but she has not replied. It would be good if Willy could come home now, before Christmas. Yours sincerely, Nancy Wajurri.

JIMMY takes one last look around his prison cell, then walks out. He leaves his prison cell then slowly walks around to the other side of the bed where he leans up on the bedhead as if it was a bar. His mood has changed.

JIMMY: I'll have a beer thanks, mate.

The chorus lean on their bedheads and order drinks one by one.

MAN: [*slurring his words*] Bros, where you from? You from 'round here?

JIMMY shakes his head but doesn't look around.

Hey, you at the bar. I'm talking to you! Where's your mob from?

JIMMY ignores him.

Hey bros, turn around. Gimme a look at that face. I seen that face before.

JIMMY: Where do you know my face from? I don't know your face, so how can you know mine?

26

MAN: [*laughing*] That's right. You don't know me but I know you. Now where do I know that face? Hey, turn around. Sis, take a look. Who's he remind youse of? Eh? I know that mob.

SIS ONE: Yeah, he's one of Nancy's mob.

MAN: That's it! He's one of Nancy's boys.

SIS TWO: That's right cuz, Nancy Wajurri.

MAN: He's the one she's been looking for, I bet. Hey bros, you here to see ya mum?

JIMMY: [*angry*] Shut up about my mother. My mother's dead.

MAN: Bros, ya mother's not dead. She's Nancy Wajurri. You must be Willy Wajurri. Eh, Willy!

JIMMY: My name's not Willy and she's not me mother. My mother's dead. So don't fuck with me. Leave me alone!

MAN: She's your mother all right. And she's been looking for ya, so's the rest of ya family. Eh! I knew I knew that face.

> JIMMY *finishes his beer and walks out while they laugh in delight at the fact that they've recognised him. Pause.*

JIMMY: Willy what? Wa-jur-ri! Willy Wajurri. Fuck me dead. [*He laughs.*] So my mother's not dead—those lying bastards. And I've got a family. It's a long time since I've seen my people. When we was kids, Mum used to tell us to look out for the men in their black cars. She was always saying—

JIMMY'S MOTHER: [*voice-over*] Be good or the Welfare'll take you. Don't hang 'round the streets or the Welfare'll take you. Don't get into no trouble or the Welfare'll take you.

JIMMY: If any cars came to the Mish we'd hide like that! [*He makes an action to show how quickly they would disappear. He laughs.*] Except one day I was in the back yard and a police car came and Mum was screaming at me to hide, but they took me and Mum was yelling—

JIMMY'S MOTHER: [*voice-over*] Let him go, let him go, let him go.

JIMMY: —I was crying and crying. They took us to Cranby Children's Home. Couple of days later—they lined us kids all up and one was chosen by this white family. I was sure someone'd come for me, but nobody ever did… [*He shakes his head.*] So I've got a mother, eh…? Fuck me! Willy Wajurri and I've got a mother!

He plonks down on the bed as if it was all too much for him.
They all sleep.

AM I BLACK OR WHITE?

ANNE: [*a little bitter*] So I finally went to meet my real mother. I thought they'd live in the country or the outback or something. You know—'at one with the land'. But here they were in a Housing Commission flat, all crowded in. I just thought it would be different, somehow.

The sheet is held up and we see the silhouette of a woman and a man, first the white parents and then black family members.

FATHER: [*off*] You're one of us, Anne—we've brought you up as one of our own.

MOTHER: [*off*] We've given you everything—a home, an education, a future.

FATHER: [*off*] Don't you appreciate all we've done?

She runs over to the other side of the stage.

FIRST BLACK VOICE: [*off*] But we're your real family.

SECOND BLACK VOICE: [*off*] Yeah, and you have to come back to us— it's where you belong, girl.

FIRST BLACK VOICE: [*off*] We lot have got to stick together, you know.

She runs back to where she began.

MOTHER: [*off*] Are you going to just throw away everything we have taught you?

FATHER: [*off*] If you go back, we won't have you here.

MOTHER: [*off*] How can you do this to us, you're breaking our hearts?

She turns away, holding her head as if in pain.

FIRST BLACK VOICE: [*off*] Of course, don't just think you have an automatic right to be here.

SECOND BLACK VOICE: [*off*] You have to earn your place if you wanna be involved in our community.

THIRD BLACK VOICE: [*off*] We wanna know who your family is, where you're from and what you've done.

Voices are crowding in on her.

WHITE VOICE: [*off*] You know nothing about them.

BLACK VOICE: [*off*] You know nothing about being a Koori.

BLACK VOICE: [*off*] Maybe ya just wanna jump on the bandwagon.

WHITE VOICE: [*off*] Maybe ya just wanna get a cheap loan or a handout.

They laugh. She's shaken and confused.

WHITE VOICES: [*together, off*] Who do you think you are?

BLACK VOICES: [*together, off*] Who do you think you are?

The voices continue to murmur 'Who do you think you are?' over and over, quietly and repeatedly. ANNE *pulls the sheet down to reveal the others.*

WHAT DO YOU DO?

JIMMY *and his mother,* NANCY/*the actor playing* SHIRLEY, *each speak alternatively, but without hearing the other.* SANDY, RUBY *and* ANNE *are singing 'Happy Birthday to You' quietly.*

JIMMY: What do you do when you meet your mother for the first time in twenty-six years? Shake her hand? Give her a hug? Do I show her me footy trophies, and me school reports?

NANCY: Twenty-six years is a long time. Gees, what if I don't recognise him? What'll I say to him?

They pull out the twenty-six presents from the box and lay them slowly on the bed.

JIMMY: Do I say, 'Hi, Mum, what's new? How have you been? Where have you been all my life?' Do I give her twenty-six Christmas presents and twenty-six birthday presents? Bloody hell, I don't even know when her birthday is…

NANCY: Maybe we'll be like strangers. Maybe he'll be ashamed of me. He probably doesn't even know how much I've missed…

She breaks down. They both hang their heads, then stand up straight as if putting on a brave face.

JIMMY: [*making a joke of it*] Hey, when you meet your mother for the first time, do you put on your best gear... or go casual?

NANCY: His foster mother's probably real smart-looking.

They simultaneously indicate their simple gear.

JIMMY: What do I tell her? Good stuff? Or all the bad stuff?

NANCY: I know I'm gunna cry...

They start putting the presents back in the box.

JIMMY: Maybe she'll wanna come and live with me and bring all the rellies.

NANCY: Maybe he'll be one of those flash blacks with a mobile phone.

JIMMY: God, I hope she's not real dirty or something.

NANCY: Will he like me?

JIMMY: She might not even like me.

NANCY: Will he love me?

The boxes go back under the bed. They stand there facing one another.

JIMMY: Will she feel like my mother...? [*Pause.*] I don't even know what having a mother feels like.

NANCY *pulls the twenty-six presents from out of the box and lays them on the floor. She takes time to consider each one, as they represent all the love she was not able to give her son.*

NANCY *collapses and dies. The presents are put back in the box or swept offstage.* JIMMY *stands happily, oblivious to his mother's death.*

I'm finally going to meet my mother.

RUBY'S FAMILY COME TO VISIT

In the dark RUBY *cries out.*

RUBY: Where are you?

The lights rise on RUBY *in the hospital bed. The chorus, representing her family, are crowded around her—they are excited to see her.*

LEN: Ruby. We're here. It's your dad Len. And your sister Joanie.

We've come a long way.

RUBY: Don't want no trouble.

LEN: Ruby, we finally tracked you down.

RUBY: Yeah... what happened to me?

They misunderstand, thinking she's talking about the past.

LEN: Well... We was real young, Ruby. They made your mum sign a bit of paper.

SISTER: She couldn't read or nothin'.

LEN: They said that she'd signed you up for adoption.

Pause.

RUBY: What happened to me...?

She indicates the institution bed.

LEN: Oh... you mean... love, you had a bit of a turn...

RUBY: [*reverting to the child, screaming*] Where are you?

LEN: We're here now, Ruby. Ruby, we wanna take you home.

RUBY: Don't live in no home any more. I work for the Hardwicks.

SISTER: Sis, we've come to take you home.

Her SISTER holds her hand, but RUBY pulls it away.

RUBY: Mmm. Don't need no trouble.

Her family stands there awkwardly while RUBY rocks and mutters to herself.

Got enough to do.

The lights go down.

SANDY REVISITS THE CHILDREN'S HOME

SANDY *walks into the space carrying his suitcase, a little lost, reminiscent of the first time he was brought to the children's home.*

VOICE: [*offstage*] Can I help you?

SANDY: Just want a look around.

VOICE: [*offstage*] If you're looking for the real estate office, it's located on the top floor. There's a display apartment there... you know they're converting this place into luxury apartments...

SANDY *wanders over to the filing cabinet. He opens the drawer and slams it with an echoey thud.*

SANDY: Luxury…

> *He gives an ironic snort. He looks around at the high walls and the bars on the windows.*

VOICE: [*offstage*] Amazing space, isn't it? This area will be the gymnasium… quality finishes… though they'll probably keep the bars, you know, to keep out the riff-raff.

SANDY: Keeping them out now…

VOICE: [*offstage*] You know this place used to be—

SANDY: [*interrupting*] I know what it used to be—

VOICE: [*offstage*] Oh.

> SANDY *takes a deep sigh, and pats his suitcase reassuringly.*

SANDY: Well, I'd best be moving…

VOICE: [*offstage*] You're not interested in an apartment?

SANDY: You've got to be joking.

> SANDY *starts to laugh, and laugh, and laugh. Fade to black.*

RACIST INSULTS

JIMMY *is drunkenly leaning on the bedhead.*

JIMMY: [*to himself*] Oh Mum, if you'd just held on a little longer…

> *Suddenly there's a voice in the darkness.*

VOICE: [*the actor playing* SANDY, *off*] You dirty black bastard.

> JIMMY *is jolted out of his drunken reverie. He sees a vision of a whitefella that no one else can see. He acts like he's about to start fighting this bloke, circling around, fists clenched and ready to swing.*

Black dog…

JIMMY: Lily white cunt…

VOICE: [*off*] Coon…

JIMMY: White supremacist…

VOICE: [*off*] Dirty nig-nog depending on government handouts…

JIMMY: Fuckin' pasty-faced fascist...

VOICE: [*off*] Bloody nigger, drinking away your dole cheque...

JIMMY: Genocidal maniac, killing and raping and stealing our women and children...

VOICE: [*off*] Hey, boong, go back to the desert where you belong...

JIMMY: Get on a boat and go back to where you came from...

VOICE: [*off*] Black bastard...

JIMMY: White bastard...

JIMMY & VOICE: [*simultaneously*] Ignorant.

> JIMMY *reels as if from a king hit, then a blue light flashes and he falls as if he were thrown. He is on the ground.*

JIMMY: [*to himself*] Black dog... scum of the earth...

> *He takes off his shoes and socks, belt, shirt, and finally necklace—each time one of the other actors comes and relieves him of the object.*

Savage... filthy black boong.

> *He stands behind the upright bed, the shadows of its base looking like bars, and his head snaps sideways as he hangs himself.*

> *A* PRISON WARDEN *(the actor who plays* RUBY*) shines a torch light on each of the beds. Bed one. Bed two. Bed three. Bed four. Bed five—*JIMMY *is hanging, swaying.*

WARDEN: Oh shit! Shit shit shit. Fuck.

> *She shines the light along the length of his body. She sees a note.*

Oh, shit!

> *The* WARDEN *shines her light on Jimmy's letter. Anger, despair, sorrow and finally resignation well up in* JIMMY *as he speaks from his noose.*

JIMMY: They kept saying she was dead...

> *Echo of voice-over saying 'Your mother's dead.'*

... but I could feel her spirit. Mum was alive and I waited and waited for her to come and get me, to take me home. I was just a little tacker, for God's sake... Dear Mum, forgive me. I have sinned. I've been a thug and a thief—but I've never stolen anyone's soul... Oh, Mum, why couldn't you have lived a bit longer just so I could meet you? I waited so long. Brothers, don't give up fighting. Don't let it happen again. Don't let them take babies from their mother's arms. Someone's gotta fight. I just can't no more. They stuck a knife into me heart and twisted it so hard. Prison don't make you tough, it makes ya weak, ya spirit just shrivels up inside. I'm going now, to be with my mother. I can't fight. I'm punched out. My only wish is that we go to the same place. Willy Wajurri.

The WARDEN *walks over and puts the letter in the file. Pause.*

WARDEN: The bastard woulda been back here anyway.

JIMMY: Maybe, maybe not.

Fade to dark.

ANNE'S SCENE

ANNE *addresses the audience, speaking to them directly.*

ANNE: S'pose you want a happy ending from me. You blackfellas want me to be reunited with my family, learn to love them, and move back home, all of us living happily ever after. You whitefellas want my adopted parents to become loving and tolerant of my black family and invite them around for a Sunday barbie—and wear badges for Reconciliation Day. Sure... Don't you? Admit it. What about me? What do I want? I don't know. I don't know where I belong any more... But hey, it's Mother's Day and I've got to make tracks. [*She pulls out a box of gift-wrapped chocolates.*] I got Mum some milk chocolates. [*She pauses, then pulls out another box.*] And I got my *mother* some dark chocolates. [*She laughs and pops one in her mouth.*] Either way, I love them both.

SHIRLEY'S COME FULL CIRCLE

SHIRLEY *stands in a beam of light at the front of the stage.*

SHIRLEY: I just met my grand-daughter—my grand-daughter. And I've decided—I want to be closer to Kate and the baby. Crikey, I'm not moving in with her or anything—I hardly know her! I've lived in the same house for eighteen years. I'll miss it, but I won't be sorry to go. They say home is where the heart is… [*Pause.*] They say time heals—but that's a load of bullshit—if you'll pardon my language. I'll tell you what heals. Holding that itty-bitty little baby. Having Kate call me Mum. The first time she did, right—we were in the hospital—she said, 'Mum, here, hold Tamara for me'—and I didn't even look up! [*Softly*] No one's ever called me Mum. Then a funny thing happened. The nurse came up and said, 'I'll take the baby now', and I said, 'No, you won't', and I burst into tears like an old fool. She just wanted to hold Tamara while Kate had a shower, for goodness' sake! The nurse must have thought I'd lost the plot. I nearly did lose the plot so many times in my life. But I didn't, and I'm glad. I have a daughter and a grand-daughter—but more important—Tamara has a mother and a grandmother. And that's all that matters.

SANDY AT THE END OF THE ROAD

SANDY *picks up his old suitcase from under his bed. He starts to walk around the room slowly as if he's going somewhere.*

SANDY: [*softly*] Been everywhere. Except one place. Home.

He wanders over to SHIRLEY.

SHIRLEY: With the grandchild. And no one's going to take her from me.

SANDY: I'm going back. Home.

He wanders over to RUBY.

RUBY: Don't need no home of me own. I've got enough to do.

SANDY: Back to me place. That bit of red desert. I still remember it. The sand must have seeped into me brain, like it did everything else. Hey! I don't have to run any more. [*With that he breaks into a trot.*] Wooha! I'm going—home.

He wanders over to ANNE.

ANNE: Either way, I love them both.
SANDY: It's calling me—home.

He wanders over to JIMMY.

JIMMY: I'm finally going to meet my mother.
SANDY: I don't have to hide. I'm going—home. And I'm gonna catch that fish!

They line up diagonally across the stage with their suitcases, just like in the first scene. Then the actors break out of their roles and talk in turn about their own experiences. Finally they leave by way of the front of the stage.

THE END

From left: Tammy Anderson, Stan Yarramunua, Pauline Whyman, Tony Briggs, Kylie Belling in the Ilbijerri/Playbox production of STOLEN, 1998 (Photo: Jeff Busby)

The tradition of storytelling is powerfully alive and well in Indigenous Australia, as witnessed in *Contemporary Indigenous Plays*—**a diverse collection of five contemporary plays from around the country.**

Adapted from her award-winning novel, **Vivienne Cleven**'s *Bitin' Back* is a 'zany and uproarious black farce' (*National Indigenous Times*) which explores stereotyping, identity and race relations in a Queensland country town.

Black Medea is **Wesley Enoch**'s richly poetic adaptation of Euripides' *Medea*. Blending the cultures of Ancient Greek and Indigenous storytelling, Enoch weaves a commentary on contemporary Aboriginal experience with 'visceral impact and lasting, disturbing imagery' (*Sydney Morning Herald*).

The acclaimed *King Hit*, by **David Milroy** and **Geoffrey Narkle**, strikes at the very heart of the Stolen Generations, exploring the impact on an individual and a culture when relationships are brutally broken.

Set in the 1950s on the fringe of a country town, *Rainbow's End* by **Jane Harrison** creates a 'thought-provoking and emotionally powerful' (*Age*) snapshot of a Koori family to dramatise the struggle for decent housing, meaningful education, jobs and community acceptance.

And **David Milroy** tells *Windmill Baby* with the poetry of a campfire storyteller and the comedy of a great yarn, amidst an abandoned cattle station in the surreal Kimberley landscape of azure skies and red dirt. Winner of the 2003 Patrick White Award, it was commended by the judging panel as 'hard as quartz, sadly poignant and hilarious all on the one page'.